EMOJIS VS.

PUNCTUATION MARKS

BATTLE OF THE KEYBOARD

MANSU EDWARDS

Emojis Vs. Punctuation Marks: Battle Of The Keyboard by Mansu Edwards Published by Mansu Edwards 1732 1st Ave #20717 New York, NY 10128

ISBN-13: 978-0-692-06845-8

A Question Mark puts his arm around a seething and bellicose Period.

"I was about to stretch off on that smiley emoticon, cheesing at my lost, he made me mad, I count to in this world," says Period.

Question Mark sighs. The Parentheses twins laugh.

"You had your day, we all did, you're just not cool anymore," yells one of the Parentheses siblings.

Period leaves the arm of The Question Mark.

"I add closure to sentences," says a defiant Period.

The Less Than symbol adds his two cents.

"You're always serious. This is a new generation and time in history. There are always memories. You're a legend", adds The Greater Than symbol.

"You know how many term papers you completed?", reminds The Question Mark.

"I feel some type of way when Danna intentionally selects an Emoji and not me. And the phone auto selects me, but, she clicks the close button to choose a Laughing Emoji", says a disappointed Period.

The Emoticons are on Danna's screen dancing and laughing while she's away from her phone.

The Thumbs Up sign picks up the Arrow symbol and points him at The Period, Parentheses and Question Mark. His knuckles shoot Laughing Emojis to tease them.

"Old symbols," says The Camcorder filming the Punctuation Marks.

"Dig a grave for these clowns," says the Bicep Emoji sign.

The Angry Emoji face says, "we can't until a developer creates it."

After saying this, the arrow strikes the asterisk in the chest. It falls down, turns white, and disintegrates into a pile of Ash.

The Delete Sign removes the ashes while the @ Sign launches a Semicolon breaking the glasses of the Intelligent Bespectacled Emoji. The curve part of the Semi-colon rupturing his cornea.

An Ambulance Emoji arrives. The Surprised and Bicyclist Emoji enter the scene. The Bicyclist sign hops off a bike and helps him into the medical van.

The Surprised Emoji rides with the victim to the hospital. The Punctuation Marks celebrate. Meanwhile, the owner of the phone, Danna is inside a laundromat holding a small bag of clothes.

She screams at her brother, Xavier for picking up her phone from the blue seat and conference calling random contacts.

The Emojis and Punctuation Marks assume their positions inside the keyboard.

"Stop, why you playing for?" screams Danna setting the clothes on the floor.

Her mother pushes a shopping cart to the spinning Dryers. It stops. And the one beside it stops. She opens the door while on the phone playing a puzzle game. Danna runs to Carla.

"Omg, they cheating, what little girl?", Carla angrily asks.

Danna stands and cries. Xavier runs around with the phone.

Carla stops. A few people watch the action.

"Hey boy, come here, you play too much, you are definitely your father's son," she says.

He stops and turns back. Xavier walks towards his sister and returns her phone.

"Why are you talking in riddles?" he asks his mom.

"Boy, if you don't....." his mother says.

The little girl opens a social app on the phone.

"I have $20,000,000. I think it'll buy me a house, that cute guy in the store and some makeup", she says.

"We're going home," says the Mother placing the final bundle of clothes in the shopping cart.

The son and daughter reluctantly follow. They exit and walk along a block of Merchants selling trinkets, socks, and Icees.

"Mama, I want a coconut one," Danna says pointing excitedly at the cart.

The Vendor smiles. Carla looks at Danna's phone.

"Close that up, I don't want you to run into something not paying attention," she says while playing games on her phone.

The little girl pouts.

"So, why are you on the phone?" Danna asks.

Carla answers without looking up.

"Little girl don't question me, I'm your mother, and I have more experience multitasking," she responds.

The little boy wanders off and fills an empty bottle in the streets with water from the hydrant and douses his sister. His mother gets a little wet.

"Boy, what are you doing and Danna put that phone away," she says all in one breath.

The girl puts the phone in her top left overall pocket.

"They sent one of ours to the hospital," rages the Embarrassed Emoticon.

Tubes are tied to The Intelligent Bespectacled Emoji's nostrils.

"I hope he makes it, is he gonna make it," asks the Angry Emoticon.

"Why you repeating those soap opera lines?" demands the Smiley Emoticon.

The Punctuation Marks are at a banquet hall. Salmon croquet and baked artichokes with marinara sauce are served by The Spacebar waiters.

The Minus and Addition symbols are watching footage of the Punctuations attack on the Emoticons on a Large Screen Emoji TV while sipping Grape Strawberry Punch.

"About time we started collecting some wins," says the Addition symbol.

The Negative sign nods.

"Oh yeah, I need to give you a check for adding another bedroom next to my two-floor living room," says the Negative symbol.

He pulls out a check.

"Where's Comma at?" asks The Addition Sign.

Comma is on the dance floor doing the Grammatical Tab Space dance with the Control, Alt and Delete female triplets.

He stops and rushes over.

"Put two commas after the o's please Sir", asks Addition.

He rises and turns into a mini comma.

"o and 2 come here", demands The Addition sign.

They come. He directs them to the check. o and 2 become smaller in size and stamp the check. The comma follows.

"Thank you, Sir, and do you still need the work done by the 18th?", The Subtraction symbol asks.

"Yes, my wife Ratio and the kids Multiply and Divide are getting antsy, they are tired of living with Grandparents Fraction," says The Addition sign.

Addition and Subtraction shake hands and continue enjoying the evening at the party. Letters X, T and C walk through the aisles dancing with White Out Pasties on their breasts.

They perform acrobatic moves on champagne soaked tables and chairs. The Suit And Tie Emoji ride a taxi carrying a microphone and camcorder.

"We've been filming since your M&A in Digital France," whines the Camcorder.

The Taxi stops at the red light. The Suit And Tie Emoji give the driver an emoticon bag of money. He leaves with the Camcorder and films the crowd outside The Punctuation Marks celebration at the Banquet Hall.

"I want to work with the Punctuation Marks, we can all get wealthier, I'm talking snatching power and control from Humans. They've been dominating us forever", The Suit And Tie, passionately explains to the camcorder as he watches the Emoji Stock Market update on the small TV next to the Emoji coin slot.

He gets a Facephone message on his tie from The Blushing Emoji.

"I'm sorry, you look so handsome in your suit, uh uh, did you find the spot?", Blushing Emoji asks

"Yes, I did, we should align with them instead of fighting them and by the way stop acting so nervous, relax it ain't that serious," he says.

She turns extra red and smiles. The Blushing Emoji ignores the first part of his message.

"I know where you are, from the live cam feed, I'll send some Ji's to help you out," she says.

Moments later, an Emoji cop car arrives. The Sgt has his head bandaged from an unforeseen altercation 15 minutes ago. His partner gets out of the car.

Punctuation Marks are leaving the venue. The Number Sign reacts violently when seeing two Emoji's jump from the front and backseat of a car with umbrellas shooting Fire and Moon Emojis.

The Asterisk sign briefly leaves his lady and jumps on his slim body. He catapults into the police car, smashing the windows. The Return Key bashes the Fire and Moon shot Emojis into the gates of a closed Punctuated Pizza Shop in the valley.

The Cops shoot two Brackets in the chest. They fall to the ground. Ink spills from their chest. Women and children scream. An Emoji Snowman arrives on an ocean wave from a helicopter circulating the Banquet's building.

The Suit And Tie watch this and jump on the ocean wave. He controls the motion and hurtles himself onto the helicopter.

"Can't make no money from chaos, I have to get out of here," he tells the helicopter.

"Mommy, my phone is hot," Danna says.

Her mother takes it from her pocket.

"That's for having it on, all the damn time, now shut it off," Carla says scowling.

The little girl turns it off. There's a power outage in the Emoji and Punctuation world. An Emoji Construction truck comes. Two workers step out and throw country flags and check signs at the banquet building.

The building shakes and slowly explodes. Punctuation Marks exit the building.

"We gotta leave, It's getting crazy out here," yells The Colon sign.

The girl's phone moves around in her pocket.

"Momma, is a phone suppose to still vibrate when the phone is off," she asks.

Carla stops and gives an angry stare.

The Bicyclist Emoji enters the scene with a flashlight. The rest of the Emojis follow and leave the scene.

"We gonna have to coordinate with the Alphabets and Numbers because we are understaffed and outmanned," says the Semicolon.

"You know they play both sides of the fence explains the Question Mark.

The Semi-Colon nods.

"They don't want to become obsolete and if they do lose power they can knock on our door or the Emoji's says The Period.

The Period, Semicolon and Asterisk travel to the Letter and Numbers town.

They go to a large phone booth. Colon dials the rotary phone. Semi-colon considers a cell phone in a glass kiosk that one can rent for $2.00 a day.

The Asterisk inserts the money into the machine, and a cell phone slides down the shoot.

Alphabet M is drawing up plans to upgrade the 26 alphabets features and functionalities.

He sends texts to Dr. Head Of Cabbage from The Land Of Refrigeration in regards to a Shape Shifter apparatus for his fellow Bets against present and future enemies.

Alphabet M then flips back to his first thought which he begins questioning.

"What if I design this and a human developer does something totally different to our features? How long will these font alterations keep us in a box? They never ask for our input. But, hey we never reached out to them, and humans think of us as inanimate images", he says.

Alphabet M drinks a cup of milk. He stares at the wall of the 7th Annual App Games between Numbers and Emojis. He gets up from the chair and looks for his pad of illustrations for the oncoming future.

"She's always moving something. I told her that this room is just for me," he steams.

M gets a text from Asterisk.

The next day, the little girl is looking in her house for her phone.

"Somebody stole my phone," she cries out from her bedroom.

"You know it's in here, stop acting like a Baby," Xavier says unabashedly.

Carla slowly walks into the bedroom with a cigarette in her left hand and a cellphone in her right hand.

"Girl, what you doing shouting like that 6:30 in the morning? No one has your phone. Hurry up and find it so you can eat breakfast and go to school", she says.

Their Dad, Menelik is on his way out the door with a briefcase. He peers into his daughter's bedroom. Menelik looks at the clothes and toys on the floor.

"It looks like someone had a fight in here, Princess are you Ok?" he sincerely asks.

"No, I can't find my phone," she says.

"Why don't you check your pajama pocket stupid?" Xavier suggests.

"Why would it be in my...." she reaches inside and finds it.

The Father smiles.

"See, you have to learn to trust people's advice," he says.

He turns to the son wearing an angry expression. The wife snickers.

"Hey Boy, watch ya mouth! You can put a spell on someone with your words", Menelik says.

"Dad, I'm a Magician?" he asks.

C'mon you're smarter than that, I'll talk to you about it later, I have to go to work", he says curling the far right corner of his mouth.

Menelik kisses his daughter and daps (fist bumps) his son. He shakes his head at Carla.

"Honey, why are you glaring at me?" she asks giggling.

Menelik leaves for work.

Later the next day, a couple of the Bets meet with the Punctuation Marks at an Organic Meditative Zen coffee shop.

"Ya'll need to peace it up or make that phone call," suggests Letter M.

Letter A folds his arms.

"You not gonna stop my money. The Emoji's brought us back to life. We make people laugh even harder with them next to us", he says.

"People weren't checking for us like that. We were just appreciated on term papers, eviction notices, bills, and kids passing notes in class", says Letter Q.

Two balls of Emoji fire enter the headquarters. The Alphabets and Punctuation Marks scatter outside. A Flashlight emoji illuminates the sky.

"We gave you money," The Angry emoji says holding a stack of bills.

The Cool Emoji holds two bags full of money.

"I thought ya'll wanted to secure the bag," adds The Buck-Toothed Emoji.

The Alphabets try to reassure the Emojis that they weren't choosing sides.

"We just want to eat like the next man. We're not warring with ya'll", explains the Letter Q.

A series of bombs float in the air and lands on the ground killing a few Punctuation Marks and Letters. The Semi-Colon and Question Mark hurls hashtags at the crew of Emojis. The tip of the tags slice lips, cut eyes and damage vehicles. The Geek Emoji blasts a sun into the sky with an innovative rocket invention. The glare burns the curvature and structure of the Bets and Punctuation Marks.

"My phone is super hot," yells Danna to her classmate, while they're doing homework on their tablets in the living room.

The phone slightly vibrates, and a bit of smoke ascends to the ceiling.

Her classmate's Father overhears her concerns while walking to the kitchen.

"Just leave it, I'll get it, It's probably an old battery that got overheated, you may need a new one," he says.

"All my classmates and important information is in there, I didn't back anything up," Danna cries.

Her classmate just looks at her.

"I'll take care of it," he says as he takes a dish towel and grabs the phone.

He places it near an open window ceil. He grabs some food from the refrigerator. There's a popping sound coming from the phone. It startles the pigeons on the ledge of the open window. They fly away. The father leaves the door open and investigates the phone.

Meanwhile, Emoji rockets continue detonating in the sky. One destroys the sun which hits the ground. It's UV light expands and intensifies, burning and blowing up Asterisk, Period, Letter M, Parentheses, Angry and Smiley Emoji and many others. Some of the Emojis jump on top of rockets to escape the light. Others hide inside destroyed Emoji cars. The sunlight quickly melts the vehicles and its victims.

One of the rockets shatters the skyline and pieces of metal obliterate the remaining cars and rockets of those Emojis, Punctuation Marks and Bets attempting to escape the mayhem. Two Emergency airplanes sponsored by Suit And Tie are deployed by The Blushing Emoji from a secret location. The surviving Emoji's, Bets and Letters hop in and land on the window ceil of the Classmate's apartment. Bits of rocket explosives and bombs sneak out the QWERTY keyboard and hit the radiator. Then there's an explosion destroying the phone's screen and the home of the Emoji's, Bets and Numbers. The Father scrutinizes the disaster.

"I'm sorry, but, you just gonna have to get a new phone," says the Father to Danna.

End Of Part 1

Author: Mansu Edwards

Email: ohassa@gmail.com

IG: MansuEdwards

Twitter: Ohassa

www.ingramcontent.com/pod-product-compliance
Lightning Source LLC
Chambersburg PA
CBHW020614130626
46552CB00007B/3205